DR. RATRICE JACKSON

www.TrueVinePublishing.org

Of Course, You Can't
Dr. Ratrice Jackson

Published by True Vine Publishing Company
P.O. Box 22448, Nashville, TN 37202
www.TrueVinePublishing.org

ISBN: 978-1-7366672-7-9
Copyright © 2021 by Ratrice Jackson

All rights reserved. No part of this book may be reproduced in any form or by any electronic or mechanical means without permission in writing from the publisher, except by a reviewer who may quote brief passage in a review.

All scripture quotations taken from the Holy Bible, King James Version, unless otherwise noted.

Printed in the United States of America—First Printing

To place orders for more books or to book the author for speaking engagements, visit: www.RatriceJackson.com

To my Grandma, Juanita:

Thank you for being an example of togetherness, faith, and peace. You have and forever will inspire me to continue using my gifts to encourage everyone around me.

TABLE OF CONTENTS:

Acknowledgments 7

Foreword 9

Advice to Leaders 13

Introduction 17

The Vision Before the Vision 23

Are you Committed? 27

Yes, I Can 36

It's Not What They Say, It's What You Believe 42

Do Something You Don't Want to Do 48

A Change Is Coming 52

The Vision Unfolding 56

What're you listening to? 63

The Art of Believing 65

Finding My Purpose 71

Be Still 77

Of Course, You Can 90

ACKNOWLEDGMENTS

I am forever grateful for everyone whom I have encountered over the years who has left an impact on me. There have been incredible spirits and prayers that have led me to where I am today. Thank you to my mom and dad, who have been the best supporters of all time. Even though I am only 5'3, I feel very tall and walk more confidently having them in my life.

Mama, you have been a stable pillar of support, you've believed in my dreams before they came into fruition, and you have never left my side. You've shown me the real meaning of support and you have become my best friend. Thank you for pushing me to be the best me I can be.

Daddy, you have always given me ways to find the light, finding the best in my situations, and have shown me the true meaning of staying strong. You have undoubtedly kept me laughing, and you always find ways to keep a smile on my face. I will never forget, during one of my highest moments in life, you would say, "Come here baby, let me pinch you to make sure this is happening for real!"

To my sister, Rachel, and brother, Ray-Ray, y'all have always been my cheerleaders who have believed in my wildest dreams. I hope and pray I have been the role model I have always aimed to be for you two. I am beyond proud to call myself y'alls sister. You both listen to me and have seen me through my good and bad, and for that I want to say thank you.

To my grandma Juanita, your beautiful soul and spirit will forever live within me. The gold rock ring that you gave Mama, I will always wear. You've shown me and exemplified the true meaning of Philippians 2:14. Thank you and I miss you. Nanny, thank you for always being so supportive. You've shined your light and have always been an active part of my life. I'll always remember you saying, *"Even though I'm shorter than you, I'll always be your nanny."*

To Mary Porter, thank you for reminding me to always "Honor Our God". You have played a huge role in my life and throughout my pivotal moments.

Lastly, to my publisher Tim. Thank you for answering the phone when God placed it on my spirit to get my message to the world through writing a book. I couldn't ask for a better publisher. The dedication that you've given me throughout my writing process and the extent that you believed in me is an experience I will always embrace. You have a gift of publishing and I couldn't be more thankful for this process.

Thank you to the many people who have modeled to me the heart of God. There are far too many people who have influenced me over the years; I would need an entire book to share their names. But those reading, you know who you are. Thank you for touching my life and molding me to be the best me that I can be.

FOREWORD

My name is Ray Jackson, Ratrice's daddy, and my wife's name is Beatrice Jackson. We took the first two letters in my name and the last five letters in Beatrice's name and came up with Ratrice. Ratrice is our first-born. I learned for the first time after we brought our bundle of joy home that I knew very little about having a newborn baby in our home. The only thing that I knew was Beatrice and I would have to wake up every two hours to feed her. I felt like I was in the military again because of the sleep deprivation. After about four months, our little angel was sleeping all night. She was a good little baby. After she was about three or four years old, we used to play catch with this rubber ball. The look in Ratrice's eyes was determination. If I received a phone call while playing catch with her and she didn't catch the ball before I answered my call, she would sit there anxiously, determined to finish so she could succeed and catch the rubber ball. I always saw that determination and strong-willed demeanor. She was also always an honor roll student in school. She made parenthood an easy task. When she started middle school, I'll never forget what happened.

She came to me and said, "Daddy, I signed up for basketball tryouts."

"Okay," I said.

Being the proud father, I was happy that our daughter was going to play sports. Her mother, Beatrice, was a cheerleader in school, so I was told many times that our daughter was going to be a cheerleader. With that being said, I asked Ratrice, "When are tryouts? Because we need to practice."

She told me, "Basketball try-outs are tomorrow."

I said to myself, "Oh my goodness, she's probably not going to make the basketball team because she has never, I mean never, played basketball in her life. She was always a girly girl."

To Beatrice and my surprise, she tried out and she made the team. Her mother and I were both happy because she played basketball with her team then, following her basketball game, she would go get dressed and come back to cheer for the boys' basketball game. I'll never forget when she came to me the following year and said, "Daddy, I don't want to cheer anymore, I want people cheering for me."

Long story short, her basketball team won the championship. She didn't return to cheerleading following that year. We also placed Ratrice in taekwondo. While in taekwondo, she won first place in the world championship within her division. What is amazing is that she had to compete against boys and girls. Beatrice and I almost couldn't believe it. Ratrice was amazingly athletic, passionate, but most of all determined. We brought home the huge trophy. Ratrice has always attained supportive friends, and many love her. One of Ratrice's grandmother's favorite Bible scriptures is, "Draw thee with love and kindness." Throughout high school, Ratrice became the vice-president of her class and also Mrs. Parkview High School. She has always been very energized about whatever project she would take on. Of course being our daughter, I could go on and on about our daughter's accolades. She always brings laughter and plenty of fun memories when we're in her presence. We're so proud of the big sister role model that Ratrice exemplifies for her younger sister, Rachel, and brother, Ray. We're very proud that our daughter loves the Lord with all her heart. To sum it up, our daughter Ratrice is intelligent, and determined to succeed and give back to society her gifts from the Lord. She is an amazing daughter and an excellent role model to her siblings. We love her dearly and we're just sitting back, watching every chapter of her lifetime book unfold. The title of this book fits Ratrice perfectly. If you tell her no, she can't do something, she will show you that OF COURSE she CAN.

We love you Ratrice,

Mama and Daddy

ADVICE FROM DR. RATRICE

Never give up, and if you have a passion for something, go for it! I believe once you live your life knowing and understanding that statement, not comparing yourself to others, and being confident, there is nothing that will be able to stop you! To live a life committed to affecting positive change within the dental field is one of my life's most important goals. More specifically, I want to focus on encouraging individuals throughout the world to keep fighting despite the hardships that they may encounter.

Three essential qualities that I believe should be kept are: perseverance, passion, and altruism. I did not make it to where I am, today, alone. I took advantage of opportunities provided to me that included internships, shadowing opportunities, and focusing on being the best me I could be. When given an opportunity, make sure you take advantage of it. Forming lifelong relationships can definitely aid in the future of your career.

Of Course, You Can't

I can't reiterate enough that when you want something, you should go for it! Despite what route God has aligned for your path, make sure you are doing everything *you can*, and God will do the rest. In terms of shadowing, seek out professionals and mentors who will take you under their wings and teach you. This will expose you to more opportunities, self-assurance, clarity of purpose, and build your confidence to succeed. Be self-assured in where you are and the lessons you have learned. Remember, passion translates to service on behalf of individuals who need it most.

Although it has not been an easy road while working to reach my goals, I am a person who does not give up despite the circumstances thrown into my path. In a world filled with many challenges, my advice to you is to use life's difficulties as a stepping stool that motivates you to keep striving for success. In life, we will all face battles, but it is up to us to persevere and continue on! It is easier to not do what you're passionate about. Not doing it takes absolutely no effort at all. What happens if you try? What happens if you don't give up on that dream? Remember, you can do whatever you put your mind to!

#OfCourseYouCan't

OF COURSE, YOU CAN'T

INTRODUCTION

"The process of getting to where you want to go is never easy. Rarely quick. But it is possible."

In the twilight of my youth, I sat upon the high hill of hope for my future and watched the sun setting. As I gaze in grateful wonder at the footprints on the landscape of my youth, I am thankful not only for my accomplishments but for the difficult experiences as well. I understand that a new day will proceed, and with it will come a new journey and new summits. For upon the setting of the next sun in my life, I know I will not be atop a hill of hope and great expectations, but a mountain at the summit of success and accomplishment, elevated to this point not because of my own power, but because of my faith, which guides me to keep climbing. My faith and religious views have inspired me to write this book.

Somewhere between hope and fulfilling a dream is someone questioning if they can do it. If you ever had this thought or simply wondered if you were alone in your journey—I wrote this book for you. The process of getting to where you want to go is never easy. Rarely quick. But it is possible. I am here to tell you that even in your wildest dreams, there's someone who looks like you who had the same hope and it led them to the unimaginable. I am that someone.

This book is for leaders, young adults, those entering into a variety of professions who may need encouragement, or simply as an example of someone that can share that similar story. I am here to motivate across the nation.

Throughout my life, I have failed over and over again. However, I have also witnessed God do the unthinkable. As I grew older, I realized that there is someone needing a book of vision who is in dental school, medical school, or any profession that may have had similar paths. For that reason, I always yearned to write a book that could be moving to that population of people. Sometimes we are not as far from the life we have imagined for ourselves as we think. Having the right attitude and faith can be that difference.

I've always had a vision to simply—tell my story. However, my story isn't as simple. As an African American young pediatric dentist from Little Rock, Arkansas, I've encountered a range of experiences amongst my career that I have continuously used for motivation. Being from Arkansas where there is no dental school, I have fought through many forms of adversity. I have been shown the impossible, and by the right attitude and faith I have changed that to *I'm possible*. Through the process, I did not understand some of the *whys* of my journey. I am just a country girl in between hope and fulfilling a dream. Sometimes the process of fulfilling the dream seems far away. If you're reading this to attain a better understanding of me, if you aspire to be inspired or if you just picked up this book to keep on your bookshelf—I 100% want to say you have selected the right one. I am here to tell more than a story, but to hopefully touch lives across the world who can relate to myself.

When comparing my countless life experiences, I often relate it to the process and journey of the game of basketball. Watching and playing basketball is my favorite pastime. Whether it is women's basketball or men's basketball, I always love to see the consistency and improvement throughout the game. There are four quarters in a basketball game. What you do in the first half determines how much work you put into the second half. However, until the buzzer goes off at the end of the game, it isn't over. That mindset has carried me into my journey of life. The way that I prepare myself daily to reach that end goal—I won! Everyone wants to see this statement but not everyone wants to do what it takes. That end goal for me is the final say that God has. A lot of times when we are watching a basketball game, it is easy to look at the stands and see one side of the stands completely full and the other side completely empty. The mindset that an audience would assume is that the other team is better and will win because it has a stand full of supporters. I want to stop you right there. I believe that mindset is false. What matters is what *you* believe. There have been times in my life where I only had about five supporters. A lot of people may look at your end goal and not realize that you *can* do it. However, I want you to know that God has the final say—keep running your race until you have reached your destination. Before you zone out, stay with me a little while longer.

Let's go back to the two teams playing basketball. Let me also state that just because one team has lost, doesn't mean that it is the end. You'll find that both effective and infective people have experienced obstacles in life of many kinds. As an effective individual, those usually are ones who use those obstacles as stepping stools. On the other hand, ineffective people will use the obstacles as excuses.

My daddy would always tell me, "Your attitude determines your altitude." During my lowest moments he would reassure me that I would be fine because I obtained the right attitude.

We have all heard that saying, right? But have we all applied it? Just as we practice before playing a basketball game or study before taking that organic chemistry final (*Whew! I remember that*), we have to practice forming good attitudes and speaking positivity over our lives. As mentioned earlier, the process of getting to where you want to go is never easy. Rarely quick. But it is possible! Each of those individuals playing on either the winning team or the losing team has a story of struggle or success, rejection or hopefulness, cynicism or potential.

Sometimes in life people attain a paradox mentality because they are afraid of growth. There is sometimes pain in the process of growth and development in order to get you to another level. Even in life, I believe encountering a variety of situations may not always be what we consider "ideal," but my philosophy on life is "pressure makes diamonds." I believe, without the pressure, we won't shine as bright as we can. Additionally, what drives me is continuously being open to learning, never settling, and always committing myself to excellence.

Hence, through the years, I have collected and compiled stories of *my* failures and successes and distilled the principles that I have learned for others in life, like you. I hope this book creates a bridge between you and me and builds up your confidence and self-worth in order for you to continue rising to the mountaintop of your future. While telling my story, I am confident that you will no longer let anything keep you from God's best. I am speaking about more fulfillment, satisfaction, and success into your life than you have ever dreamed. Don't wait any longer—keep climbing.

THE VISION BEFORE THE VISION

Have you ever sneezed so hard that you close your eyes so tightly and suddenly see black stars? There's a sudden expansion in the chest, your lungs are filled with air then you let it out with a loud outburst of "Achoo!" The same uncontrollable and involuntary experience occurred January 2008 on a cold Wednesday afternoon. There was a cracking pop that echoed amongst the gymnasium as I held my left knee on the basketball court. My veins intensified, as I could no longer extend my leg.

Oh my God! What just happened? I thought. My knee immediately began swelling. It was so huge. It looked like there were two golf balls in my knee.

The black stars floated above my head as my daddy picked me up and rushed me to the car. My leg felt like it was dangling like a twig in the wind.

"Hold my leg! Daddy" I screamed. I honestly believed my leg was going to fall off.

Daddy rushed me to the vehicle and put the pedal to the metal. Tears flowed down my face but not as much for the pain. I was more devastated that I would be out for the season.

"Oh my God, Mama! How long do you think I'm going to be out for the season?"

"Girl, you need to worry about your knee, not the basketball season," Mama corrected me.

I don't remember much about that trip. I just remember being in that cold, white hospital room.

***

"Is it Ruh-Treece?" the doctor asked.

"No Sir, it is Ray-Treece," I corrected him.

"Oh what a beautiful name," he exclaimed.

I proceeded to explain to him, "My dad's name is Ray and my mom's name is Beatrice. So, they combined their names to make mine."

The doctor laughed and said, "Very unique, very unique."

There was an abrupt pause and he proceeded, "Well, Miss Ratrice, you have a torn ligament in your knee. This is something we can treat using physical therapy. I know you're a senior. What are your plans in life?"

What were my plans? I was looking at my life plans fade before my eyes. I gasped in disappointment about the idea of not playing basketball anymore. I felt broken and devastated. Sitting there in that emergency room, it took everything within me to hold back my tears. I never liked crying in front of my parents. I always carried a persona of toughness. I believed that in order to be tough, you didn't cry, but as I sat on the stretched seat in the emergency room, I felt empty. I am not sure if you can imagine how this feels, but for me it felt like being thirsty and looking at an empty cup.

I thought to myself, *what are my other passions?*

My mama would always tell me that I was talented and that God knew what was best, but I could not comprehend any of this because I didn't know. I didn't know what else I was good at. I knew that I was in school because it was the right thing to do, but there were so many thoughts that went through my mind. I did not know what was next for me or if I would ever find a love like I had for the sport of basketball. I sat there with a swollen knee and overheard the doctors tell my parents that I would be on crutches for weeks at a time and would be undergoing physical therapy.

I know that everyone does not have this challenge of figuring out their passion and waiting until it is revealed. Everyone who knows me knows that I am always smiling and laughing. Until high school, I would get in trouble at school for laughing so much. Everything was always funny to me or I would always find humor in situations, but the humor and spark inside of me died in that moment of not knowing what else that I wanted to do.

There I was, a senior in high school with no basketball, and no clue about what I wanted to do. I kept thinking of ways to get back on the court, but in the back of my mind, I knew that a 5-foot-3-inch woman with a bad knee was not going to find her way into the WNBA. I felt so lost and struggled with the pressure of being the oldest child. I was supposed to be the trailblazer to show my younger siblings the way, and yet my future looked bleak.

It felt like everyone was getting ahead of me because "they" knew what they wanted to do in life. It seemed like "they" had everything figured out. You know how it goes—everyone is always worried about what "they" are doing. Still to this day, I have no idea who "they" is. My mama would always ask me, "Who is 'they'?"

Little did I know this place of brokenness, confusion and asking, "Why me?" was leading me to a vision bigger than I'd imagined. I called it *The Vision before the Vision.*

Have you ever had to overcome brokenness? What was your response? How did you handle brokenness throughout your life? What exactly *is* the state of being broken? I have learned that brokenness is a necessary, yet temporary state of being that camouflages itself as hurtful when actually it is helpful. I have learned through my journey that it is in this broken state that God sets us aside and works on us in ways that we never would have allowed Him to when we were whole. Consequently, when you get back into the race, you will run faster, be stronger, wiser, and you will be more resilient. Whether that's a failed examination, a delay in a hopeful dream, a bump in the road that we as humans see as a hindrance—God uses it all for our good.

ARE YOU COMMITTED?

Following my injury, over time, a strange thing happened. Instead of being discouraged, I became more inspired than ever. It was refreshing for me to have this new challenge of discovering myself. I am a super ambitious person, so I was looking at different avenues that sparked my interest. I get this passion from my roots.

My grandmother, Juanita Owens, was always a prayerful, optimistic, virtuous woman of God. I like to say that she reminds me of the scripture, "Proverbs 31: She is clothed with strength and dignity; she can laugh at the days to come. She speaks with wisdom, and faithful instruction is on her tongue." My grandmother's personality translated to my mother. My mom is a praying woman. She speaks positivity over my life and has been a constant reminder of keeping the faith and staying resilient. Hence, when thinking of core values, commitments and beliefs that drive me as an individual, I think, firstly, about my upbringing.

So, it was no surprise that I initially wanted to go into the field of ministry. Later, I started watching episodes of Judge Judy and imagined going to law school. My mother was a manager at UPS, so I thought about studying business. Perhaps I could be a corporate leader like my mama, I figured. I even thought *maybe I'll be an actress* and even got my big break when I was cast for a commercial for The University of Arkansas at Fayetteville. But I just couldn't find the right fit.

Trying to find your purpose and passion can be exhausting. I always thought to myself, *is it always this hard? Do people usually go on a hunt for their passion?* It just didn't seem normal to me. Even though I didn't know what I wanted to be, I still needed to get into college. My leg injury gave me the time I needed to search for scholarships, since I was no longer spending my time at basketball practice. I applied for dozens of scholarship opportunities.

One scholarship in particular changed my life. After applying for so many scholarships, I received a letter in the mail. The envelope was large and had a pink and green return label that read Alpha Kappa Alpha Inc. of Arkansas with my name addressed on it. The envelope was already opened because my mama always opens my mail, for some reason.

She came into my room with a smirk on her face and said, "Here, this is for you."

I was so confused. Not because of the envelope package, but because I just never understood why she always opened my mail when it said my name on it. I opened it, looking curiously at my mom who was smiling ear to ear. I actually forgot that I'd applied for this scholarship because I'd applied for so many, but I was excited to see my first response.

I had sent so many with no response that I was beginning to wonder if people actually looked at scholarship applications, or was it all some big joke? I never knew anyone lucky enough to receive a scholarship. This was all new to me, but I took a shot at it to find out.

I pulled out the sheet of paper inside. The letterhead was emblazoned with a beautiful green ivy leaf.

"This is so pretty," I said. I knew absolutely nothing about sororities but seeing the pink and green letterhead was very enticing.

My mother's excitement was spilling over. My whimsical pace was driving her crazy.

"Focus baby! Read it!" she blurted.

"Okay!" I laughed.

My eyes fell on a bold, "**Congratulations!**"

I was one of the scholarship recipients, but they wanted to interview me to confirm the final scholarship award offer.

I was confused.

"Why do I have to interview for a scholarship?" I asked my mom.

"I don't know, girl, but you better go so you can get that money because you know I'm not paying for your school!" She walked away with a chuckle to tell my dad what was going on.

"Hey Ray! Your daughter is about to be off of our credit line because she's getting scholarships so we can now have more money in our pockets." They both laughed.

"I'm happy for you baby! Keep it up because I like all of my money, so you need to get yours."

The night before the interview I wanted to make sure my clothes were ironed. I didn't know what to wear so I ironed three different button-down shirts. I had this black skirt suit that I'd had for years, but I never wore it because I had nowhere to wear it. That morning, everything was ironed but I did not know which shirt to wear. Remembering the pink and green on the piece of paper, I thought to myself *oh, I am going to wear the pink button-down shirt.*

I wore this pink shirt every chance I got.

My mom would always tell me, "I am going to throw that shirt away. People are going to think that you don't have any other clothes to wear because you wear it every Sunday."

I didn't care that I wore it all of the time because that was my favorite shirt. When I really like something, I wear it a lot. I don't care about fashion rules. I'm a practical girl who likes what I like.

I was anxious, nervous, and excited that morning. Anxious to find out how much my scholarship would be, nervous about messing up the interview, but excited about the entire process. I didn't know what to expect.

When I arrived, a dignified woman stood at the entrance dressed in a black skirt suit wearing a beautiful white pearl necklace and bracelet. She greeted me and escorted me to the conference room for the interview. She exuded confidence. I always felt like I was a confident person, and I felt like I could see myself in her.

Who is this woman? I thought. *I wonder what she does for a living.*

As we approached the conference room, my nerves went crazy. I began focusing so much on what kinds of questions I would be asked in the interview that I tripped over my heels while walking into the room.

After regaining my composure, I looked up to find six more of these dignified, confident women in black suits and pearls sitting at a conference table, staring at me. This entire time I'd thought I would be meeting with one person. I usually don't get nervous, but I started to sweat.

What an embarrassing entrance. I laughed and recomposed myself.

"Good morning; I guess you won't forget who I am after this entrance," I said.

We all laughed as I took my seat at the head of the table. All eyes were on me and the smiles disappeared as we moved to the business at hand.

As intimidating as the interview was, this process was like a light in a dark tunnel leading me to my destiny. It was during this interview process that I realized that this world is full of amazing and talented women who had the same feelings that I had. They didn't know the exact path or direction that they wanted to go down at my age, either. The women that honored me with their scholarship award encouraged and affirmed to me that I was not as lost as I believed myself to be.

They helped me to understand that at 17, it was okay if I didn't have my life planned out perfectly. They told me that I had time to figure out my ultimate plans but told me that I was on the right track. It was the guidance I needed. I know a lot of times in life at 17 years of age or even at 37 years of age, we expect to have everything figured out, and if we don't we feel that we are behind. There's no timeframe on success and figuring out your passion. Also, it's never too late. I realized later in life that everyone's journey in life is similar to trying on a t-shirt. You can try on the next person's t-shirt, but if it's not the right size then it won't fit. We all have different paths and journeys, and it is okay to take the time to figure out the direction for you.

The dark path would become brighter that summer. I was attending a program called Arkansas Commitment. My mom entered me into this program my sophomore year. This program had a primary mission to assist young African American students in acquiring the knowledge, skills, and professional experience necessary for effective community leadership. Many qualities that are essential to the goal of this program are instilled in me still, and have molded a foundation for hard work and dedication.

I attended every Saturday rain, sleet or snow. For me, it wasn't until after my injury that God began to show me the direction and path set aside for me through this program. After regaining my passion and accepting God's plan for my life, even though I couldn't see it myself, my eyes were open to many experiences that I am not sure I would have appreciated without my knee injury.

Participating in this phenomenal program taught me the value of staying *committed*. I remember like yesterday the first Saturday of the month, the sound of the 8:00 am alarm going off. My mama would always come down to my room and pull the covers from over my head to awaken me. Knowing her weekend routine, I would hastily place the blankets back over my face to avoid getting out of bed.

"But Mama, it is Saturday," I protested.

"Get up! It's time for Arkansas Commitment," she would exclaim while quickly turning the lights on.

Releasing the blankets from over my face, I stretched and yawned with a loud gasp. I was unaware of the influence of this program until years later. I'll never forget being selected to interview on a panel of individuals for an internship position. Based on this interview, the panel placed the interviewee in an internship where they felt we would be most fulfilled. After the selection process, I received an internship in a dental office, and I was also doing research on childhood obesity at Arkansas Children's Hospital.

I drove home confused about their selection, but excited to share the news with my mom.

"Mama, I am going to be in a dental office. Can you believe that?" I shouted with glee. You could see the happiness on my mom's face. I turned around and rhetorically asked, "Did you pray for this?" as we both chuckled.

On the first day of my internship, I walked in and an African American male approached me and said, "Hey there, I am Dr. Samuel Wofford. Are you Ratrice?"

I was very puzzled because I had never seen an African American physician, let alone an African American dentist.

I replied, "Yes, I am." I was very excited yet nervous, because being in a dental office was an extremely new feeling for me. I am a very observant person — and I mean extremely observant. My mom tells me all of the time that I am way too nosy, and I laugh and tell her, "Mama, I am very observant."

So, as I approached Dr. Wofford's office, I looked around at all of his accolades. The very first one that I saw was, "Doctor of Dental Surgery Degree from Meharry Medical College School of Dentistry in Nashville, Tennessee." I turned around and asked him,

"Muh-Haw-Ree is in Nashville?"

He quickly corrected me, "Muh-hairy is in Nashville, yes."

"I have never heard about Meharry," I replied.

He gave me a run down that included Meharry Medical College being chartered separately in 1915. Also, in the early 21st century, it had become the largest private historically black institution in the United States solely dedicated to educating healthcare professionals and scientists. I was amazed because at 17, I was unaware that this was a.... possibility.

Being able to have a new dream that transpired from a knee injury to a possibility of becoming a black female dentist was unheard of. At least, it was for me. We don't have a dental school in Arkansas, which meant applying for out-of-state schools would make it even more competitive. Nonetheless, I knew after months of interning that this was a dream that I did not want to give up on.

I wasn't sure how I was going to get to the destination, but I knew by faith that God would order my steps. The very last day interning with Dr. Wofford, he gave me a printed black and white piece of paper. Back in the day, colored printing was too much, as we were very conservative. We also used a film developer where we had to go into a dark room to develop our own radiographs. We live in a microwave society where I am sure every office has now switched over to digital, but that just gives you a background of how times have changed. This black and white printed sheet of paper was entitled, "The Summer Medical and Dental Educational Program." I folded the piece of paper and put it in the glove compartment of my 2009 white Toyota Camry, affectionately named La Pearla.

There was a little voice in my head that whispered, "Stay Committed". As I finished my internship and headed to college, I would challenge myself and ask, "Are you Committed?"

YES, I CAN

In 2009, I was driving to school when I heard an advertisement on the radio. Power 92 Jams was hosting Burger King's "Yes, I Can Achieve Essay Contest." The requirement was to write an essay about the barriers that existed within the United States and how I planned to overcome these barriers to achieve my goals. The winner of this contest would win a free laptop for college.

After my knee injury, my daily focus was applying to as many scholarship opportunities as possible. Developing and growing constantly requires adaptation, and since a basketball scholarship was no longer on the cards for me, I was determined to make the best of my new condition. As soon as I got home, I went straight to my computer and started typing my essay. Although I was a little intimidated, I forced myself to follow through. I concluded that although I could not control the outcome, I could control my effort.

I sat down, took a deep breath and began to type:

"Yes, I Can Achieve

My much-loved Thoreau quote, 'Go confidently in the direction of your dreams, live the life you have imagined,' are words I live by. Lack of free medical clinics, children without insurance, elderly adults who cannot afford their medications are disparities that exist within the United States of America that I have seen first-hand in my hometown of Little Rock. Working as an intern at Dr. Wofford's dental office and also being an intern at Arkansas Children's Hospital has made me aware at an early age of our nation's cry for help within its many underserved communities. There is an urgent need for selfless individuals who possess a steadfast desire to aid others. Every day I am reminded of America's specific need for assistance, and this is what sparked my drive to pursue a career in primary healthcare.

Through Arkansas Commitment, I was able to take part in the Coordinated School Assessment Study funded by the Arkansas Biosciences Institute. The study included disadvantaged middle schools in Arkansas. My objectives were to evaluate the impact of the school's atmosphere and the underprivileged environment on children's risk for overweight status. After a year of participating in this study and as a result of my high-quality performance, I was asked to take part in the exceptional Arkansas Children's Hospital Childhood Obesity Prevention Research Program, the Delta Garden Study. The Delta Garden Study has a mission to strengthen community resources, volunteerism and national service in Arkansas. This study was designed to prevent childhood obesity and social risk behaviors in middle school children living in the disadvantaged Delta and Central regions of Arkansas. It is the largest, and most scientifically rigorous, school garden research study in the nation. My job as an intern prepared me to work with underserved populations.

Through my experiences, I realized that there are three essential qualities that I sought and continue to seek daily: perseverance... passion... altruism.

This career path that I decided to take requires steadfast hard work and clear focus within the academic setting. These same qualities must be demonstrated in the workplace, as a healthcare professional works to cure patient sicknesses and bring patients back to good health. Therefore I believe, as privileged and educated Americans, we cannot continue to turn our backs on the people who need us the most. I have always wanted to contribute all in my power to help create a better America and a world for underserved communities. I encourage you to possess perseverance, passion, and altruistic endeavors in whatever it is that you want to do in life.

Dr. Martin Luther King Jr. once said, "Freedom is never voluntarily given by the oppressor; it must be demanded by the oppressed." We are an oppressed people if we cannot embrace our own heritage and win this war. So I say, **"Yes, I can! Yes, I will!"***"*

A few weeks later, I got a phone call.

"Hello?" I answered.

"This is Broadway Joe from Power 92 Jams, the people's station. May we speak with Miss Ratrice Jackson?"

As I grabbed my crutches and walked outside, I responded, "This is she."

"Ratrice, congratulations! You have just won a laptop for your submission to Burger King's "Yes I Can Achieve Essay Contest," Broadway Joe exclaimed.

I was asked to talk live at the Power 92.3 radio station in my community of Little Rock, Arkansas. As I approached the address and listened to what was being played on the radio, I heard the announcement,

"We are going to have Ratrice Jackson come talk to us live about her 'Yes, I can achieve essay' and we also have Burger King here. Stay tuned!"

I thought to myself, *I can do whatever I put my mind to. Yes, I Can!*

***

I want you to think of a moment in your life where you were hit with the passion and desire to carry out your dreams but battled with insecurity and second-guessing yourself. You may even be dealing with this right now. I know you think you are the only person experiencing this emotion, but believe me, you are not. Just as I believed the world was passing me by, I soon learned that several women had gone through the same doubts.

I don't deny that these may be difficult times. I don't expect you to suddenly become Mr. or Ms. Confidence after reading this story. However, I do want you to believe in yourself more than you believe in your fears. Believe that one ounce of effort will move you closer to your dream than standing idle in fear. Be willing to take baby steps. No one said following your dreams would be easy. However, remember that you don't have to do it all at once. Instead, take incremental steps towards your faith, and your vision will become clearer as you continue to believe.

I didn't know how I would pay for college, but I took one step at a time; one scholarship application and essay at a time. I did not receive every scholarship for which I applied, but by applying to as many scholarships as I could, I was able to pay for my education.

Perhaps your circumstances are different. Maybe you've lost your job and are seeking a new career. Maybe you are still unsure of what you want to do at this moment. This is not always a bad part in life. Sometimes we consider these experiences a setback in the moment, but they are actually a set up by God for something greater. Don't let the circumstances of your life dictate where you want to be.

I always say that the mind is more powerful when you learn how to direct it. Shift your mindset from a place of disappointment and direct it towards productivity, positivity, and determination. Do at least one thing that could move you closer to the life of your dreams. If you're looking for a new job, send an application. If you're wanting to start a new business, get your business license. There is always something you can do to build momentum.

This is not always easy. I mean, do you really just jump out of bed in excitement when you're disappointed and when your plans didn't turn out the way that you expected them to? *Of course* not! Learning how to direct your mind can be as challenging as this. Redirecting your mindset is similar to getting into a workout routine. When you're working out and your legs get tired you push yourself to get in those last two reps. Why? You push yourself for three reasons:

First, you know that your efforts have an appointed end. If you didn't know when your workout would end, you would probably be less likely to push yourself. However, because you know the exact number of reps you want to accomplish, you can push yourself even when it hurts. When pursuing your goals, you need to set benchmarks of success. Sending 10 applications per week or giving out 15 business cards a week, for example. These definitive, quantifiable goals give you the sense of accomplishment and the frame of reference to keep you moving forward.

Secondly, you believe the exercise will benefit you. When you believe that your efforts will be of benefit and lead you closer to your dreams, you will work with more vigor and confidence because you understand that the sooner you finish, the sooner you will accomplish your goal. If I told you that if any person can receive the job of their dreams after submitting 1000 applications, how many applications would you submit each day? Most people give up after a few rejections because they are focusing on the outcomes instead of the exercise. The exercise of success consists of the mundane steps we take that no one sees. It consists of the books we read, the rejections we endure, and the failed attempts. Those who give up, stop believing that the exercise is beneficial. However, if you continue to believe in the benefits of exercise, before you know it you'll take a look in the mirror and see a different person.

Lastly, you push yourself because you have a clear vision of what the exercise will accomplish. Would you go through the pain of doing sit-ups if you didn't believe it would make your abs look stronger? Would you do 100 push-ups hoping to build your leg muscles? *Of course* not. When you have a clear idea of how you want your body to look, you will exercise the specific muscle needed to create your vision. Likewise, when you have a clear vision of how you want your life to look, you will have greater clarity on what steps you need to take to make it a reality. So take the time to create that crystal-clear vision and identify the efforts needed to bring that vision to reality.

When you apply this approach to your goals and challenges, you will direct your mind to believe, "*Yes, I Can.*"

IT'S NOT WHAT THEY SAY, IT'S WHAT YOU BELIEVE

Walking the campus of The University of Arkansas at Fayetteville, I felt misplaced. Misplaced because this was my first time away from home. I'd worked my butt off and got a full scholarship into college. I had big dreams, but I felt so far away. I would call my mom and dad every second that I could. I didn't really know anyone on campus. This was going to be tougher than I expected. I was between hope and fulfilling a dream.

In 2009, I learned that I wanted to go into the health professional field. I allowed my journey to show me signs about what I should do. As I started my new journey, I met up with my advisor and explained to her my vision of applying to dental school and inquiring about the steps that I needed.

"Do you have a Plan B?" she asked.

This statement confused me.

Is she trying to convince me to give up on my goal? I've been here for two minutes and she wants me to quit already?

"I do not have a Plan B but I am confident that I will do fine with classes as long as I am being guided in the right direction," I said, subtly reminding her that her job was to give me direction on how to achieve my goals, not talk me out of them.

The advisor went into detail explaining the courses that I would have to take; almost too much detail. It was as if she was trying to info-dump-- that's when someone piles so much information on you that you become confused and overwhelmed. The advisor started telling me about the challenges of General Chemistry and Organic Chemistry.

"These are the 'weed out' classes," she said smugly. "These classes determine if someone will succeed further in this field."

I had a puzzled look on my face, because I was not sure what her goal was.

"Well. Thank you for your advice and I am sure that I will do well," I said with a courteous, albeit fabricated smile. I wanted her to know that I was determined to succeed no matter how much she tried to discourage me.

***

Just because you have big dreams for yourself does not mean everyone does. There are those who want to see you fail or underachieve for a number of reasons: racial bias, jealousy, personal ambitions, or maybe they were just in a bad mood. Who knows why? Therefore, it is important that you speak life over yourself at all times and believe only in that which you want to manifest.

I have always stood by the biblical scripture:

'Proverbs 18:21: "The tongue has the power of life and death."

The stakes are high. Your words can either speak life, or your words can speak death. Our tongues can build others up, or they can tear them down.'

If you have had doubts or had anyone doubt you, just know, "It is not what they say, it is what you believe!" I understand that this statement is more than a notion, and situations are not always favorable. However, at the end of the day, what you believe will take you further than what statistics show.

It is important that we become aware of the roots of our self-talk. Self-talk is your internal dialogue. It's influenced by your subconscious mind, and it reveals your thoughts, beliefs, questions, and ideas. Self-talk can be both negative and positive. I believe that being aware and reflecting on the way that we think is extremely essential, especially when we are encountering transformations in life.

The core of our beliefs actively translates to our perspective in life. When I am having thoughts of uncertainty, I alter my mindset to believe the positive. Three practices that work best for me are:

1) Meditation

Meditation comes in different ways for everyone. Sometimes it's hard to find that form of meditation. I know your mind can drift to a form of soft music, yoga, or even sleep. I alter my mindset through talking to myself on what brings me comfort. That simply could be sitting still in a room and doing breathing exercises. This doesn't automatically change my disposition or situation, but it helps me to attain a view of focusing on the positive and appreciating the moment that I'm in. It has taught me how to transform negative thoughts out. Of course this is easier said than done, but I do find it is helpful to alter my mindset to believe the positive. This doesn't happen overnight. Sometimes it takes me a few days or even weeks to allow myself into a space of peace. Be easy on yourself and kind to your body. Adding meditation has helped me become more at peace and clearer on my thoughts.

2) Prayer

For me, praying is truly believing that there is a way, even when it looks like there is no way to be made. I have always heard the saying, "Pray about it and get some rest." Years later, I realized that this simply meant believing that God has it under control and trusting His process. I talk to God just like I talk to a friend. In times of uncertainty, I will pray and tell God how I am feeling and what is affecting me in that moment. I don't pray simply when things are not going well, and that's the key. So how do you pray? How does this help with my uncertainty? I pray and give thanks for everything that God has brought upon my life, and I also pray for discernment on what is not clear. My mindset is not immediately altered with one prayer but, for me, it helps bring my mind calmness to know that my situation is in the hands of someone greater than me. Meditation is linked to prayer for me, because I am able to bring myself into a moment where there is silence and stillness while pushing myself ever so slightly to believe the positive.

3) Talk to a trusted friend or mentor

For me, my family has always been the centerpiece of altering my mindset to believe in the positive of my situation. I understand that some may not have the positive door to go straight to and change your perspective with. There have been times in my life where I have felt as though no one understood the situation that I was going through. I learned early on that holding in my stress is not healthy. I would have a sudden outburst and not understand why and where it had come from. I have had a good experience sharing my situation and seeking mentorship in a personal counselor and a therapist. This has been helpful in altering my mindset to believe the positive.

Now, I am not saying to not use your forms of difficulty as a stepping stool and learn from different experiences, but I am simply sharing that it is okay to have opposition as long as we keep our heads high and continue speaking greatness over our lives.

It's not what they say; it's what you believe.

DO SOMETHING YOU DON'T WANT TO DO

In the words of Mark Twain, "Do something every day that you don't want to do. This is the golden rule for acquiring the habit of doing your duty without pain."

Style as we know it is a manner of doing something. I was a very determined person, which has helped me throughout my life. But there have been a lot of moments where I've had to do something that I didn't want to do. While in school, I knew that I didn't always have the energy to stay up late to study or even wake up early, but I knew that I couldn't give up. This was just the beginning.

Let's go back to La Pearla. She gave me the agreement that I could discuss her as much as I wanted throughout my book, so I told her that I would hold her to her word. When La Pearla gets dirty, I like to take her to get a car wash. During this time, a year after my internship, I decided to clean my glove department of my vehicle. My car was parked right outside of my parents' house and there it was--a faded black and white sheet of paper that I mentioned in the chapter, "Are you committed?" I could barely see the ink on the paper, but it read "SMDEP." The faded remnants of the lettering made me soon recall it being given to me by Dr. Wofford. I instantly applied to this program as it was evidence that this was a sign. Shortly after, I took La Pearla to the car wash. Imagine going through a car wash and seeing the different soaps and waxes sprayed all over. You are not quite sure as to when the car will be finished being washed, but all that you know is that your car is going to come out clean. This same concept applies throughout life, which I often remind myself of. Sometimes we are only getting a little cleaned up in order to be prepared for the next destination assigned for our life.

Summer of 2011, I was accepted into The Summer Medical and Dental Educational Program (SMDEP). I was accepted into three sites: Yale University, The University of Washington in Seattle, and The University of Louisville, Kentucky. I decided to accept the position at The University of Washington. This program is a summer enrichment program, focused on improving access to information and resources for college students interested in the health professions. SMDEP's goal is to strengthen academic proficiency and career development of students underrepresented in the health professions, and prepare them for a successful application and matriculation to health profession schools.

The duration of this program allowed me to get a head start on courses such as biology, general chemistry, and organic chemistry. Additionally, I was able to shadow different specialties of dentistry such as a research dentist, oral maxillofacial surgeons and general dentists. That was a challenge because I remembered that my advisor had told me the classes that I sought were 'weed out' classes.

Throughout this program, I struggled with grasping the material for general chemistry and organic chemistry. I instantly thought, *maybe my advisor is right*, but the other side of my brain was ready for the challenge.

Of Course, You Can't

Throughout this 8-week program, I made sure that I wrote down my goals. There was an idea brought about during this program that has stuck with me. The instructor noted you to write down your goals for the year. Break down your goals into four different dates; usually broken down into seasons. Place each piece of paper in an envelope and do not open it again. The idea was to mail the envelope to yourself around the date set aside to reach the goal. This challenged the mind to achieve your goals and to not give up. In this moment of preparation for the road ahead of applying to dental school, regrettably, I still felt a bit discouraged.

There are many of you on the same road, and suddenly you may feel discouragement because of what you are seeing in front of you. Any time I reach that moment, I always remind myself of faith. I ask myself, do you have faith? Then I realize that we all have faith in some capacity. Think about it. I bet you a dollar against a donut that you walked somewhere today, whether it was your room, living room, a barber shop or even the kitchen table, and sat down. Now, did you think to yourself before sitting down if the chair was going to break? Did you check underneath to see if the screws were still in or if it would move once you sat? I am certain 99% of people would answer no to that question. Why? Because you believed that the chair was not going to break. Many of you never even thought about if it was going to break or if it was stable - you just sat down. I use these correlations because when we are applying our faith to our ambitions, why do we think about our failures before we even approach the idea of success? We have seen many people fall out of chairs or sit in a broken chair, but we never remind ourselves of that moment when we sit down. The same concept applies to our daily walk in life. I say daily because I decided at an early age to train my mind and subconscious to believe and speak the good before being accustomed to the worst-case scenario.

Don't get me wrong - we will have failures in life, and we will have learning moments, but I challenge you today to use those moments to endure your naysayers. Most times, your cynic happens to be the little voice in the back of your head. We all have that little voice that speaks to us daily.

Instead of thinking, *Omg, what if my advisor is right, what if I fail these weed out classes?* I changed the little voice to say, *I know these are weed out classes but I'm possible.* I had to remind myself that the process of getting to where you want to go is never easy, rarely quick, but it is possible. I did not fully understand my style in life at an early age; however, through the years, I was shown that my style included spreading positivity through my daily reminders to myself and to others. Each of us maintains a style that follows us. Hopefully, I have inspired you to willingly self-examine and allow your style to gear you in the direction of staying the course of your hopes and dreams. I call this *stylish excellence.*

A CHANGE IS COMING

"You must be the change you want to see in the world." -- *Ghandi*

The purpose of Gandhi's statement, I believe, was to help people to understand the *"why"* of their existence. Why do you wake up in the morning? Why do you work very hard? Why do you make the decisions that you make?

In college, I constantly asked myself these same questions while chasing my dream. This was not a practice of insecurity and uncertainty. It served as a daily reminder and motivation to push for greatness. The answers to your life are found in your questions. Thus, when you ask yourself, "Why?" you get more clarity on the how.

I gained more clarity on my goals and the people, resources, and opportunities I needed to achieve my goals. I applied to numerous internships and educational programs, just seeking to find my place. I sought out and found individuals who could help me. You must understand that your dream and your goal is a 'pursuit.' The word 'pursuit' is defined as 'the action of following or pursuing someone or something.' I hope you caught that powerful word – 'action.'

Pursuing your goal is an action. You must take action. The people you need will not come to you. The opportunities you need will not appear out of thin air. The resources you need will not seek you; you must actively seek them. You must accept that you will be rejected, denied, blind-sided and all of the scary things that cause you to hesitate. Yet after the bumps, bruises, and embarrassment, you will be that much closer to your destiny.

My opportunity came when I was accepted into a program called "Profile for Success" at The University of Michigan School of Dentistry.

The purpose of Profile for Success (PFS) was to assist college students and recent graduates through the admissions process for dental school. PFS targeted individuals making a career transition who were on track to enter dental school the academic year following their participation. Preparation for the Dental Admission Test (DAT) was the main focus of this program.

While at this summer program, I spent my time writing out my goals and appreciating the process. The most powerful vibration we can emit is the vibration of gratitude and appreciation. We must show excitement for the good, the bad, and the mundane. These are all quintessential components in your journey to success. When you maintain a spirit of gratitude and excitement, you attract the positive results you desire.

I had goals of getting high scores on examinations and goals of meeting and befriending influential leaders who could help me. This positive expectation led me to meeting a friend along my journey. Her name is Daria. We instantly connected and I told her my goals. I also mentioned that I was nervous about the competitiveness of dental school. I explained to her that I would have to really stand out, because I was applying to all out-of-state schools since there were no dental colleges in my home state.

"I wish Arkansas had a dental school for their residents," I complained.

Daria stopped me at that moment and said, "Trice, increase your faith."

I was startled. I paused, because in that moment I realized I needed to do what I had been preaching to others and apply it to my own life. Can you imagine what I felt at that moment? My paradigm shifted. Suddenly I saw things differently.

It is always easier for the mind to expose why you can't do something. It is human nature. We must intentionally shift our minds to believe that we can achieve. When you believe that you *can't* achieve, you will give up when hard times come. How many times are we saying to ourselves about what we can't do because of the opposition that we are facing? When you give up, you fulfill your own prophecy. However, when you believe you *can* achieve, you will push through the difficulties to find the solutions needed for your success and fulfill your own prophecy. The question is, which prophecy would you like to fulfill: the prophecy of failure or the prophecy of success?

***

When I completed the dental admission test, my score did not reflect my goal. That's right - I was emitting gratefulness and gratitude, I was speaking faith and positivity, I was doing everything right, and I did not succeed.

I'm going to let that rest in your mind for a second…

I was not sure what I was going to do at this point. I was doing all that I could do and still it was just not good enough. I know you have felt that before. You put in so much work and effort and it seems like the world does not see it. It seems as though in that moment, you see everyone else succeeding or accomplishing what *they* want to in life. I absolutely knew that I would have to retake the examination in order to get accepted into a dental program.

I reached out to my main supporters, crying and discouraged. They told me that everything I needed would come in due time, if I just didn't give up. They gave me the jumpstart I needed. I knew that I had a goal and I wasn't going to let anything stop me from achieving the vision. I knew that a change was coming.

As a result, Gandhi's statement written that I believe to be true has opened up an essential approach that will enable mankind to begin their journey to an open mind. That approach is that although life changes are inevitable, we can also initiate personal change so we can rise to the challenge and become a bigger and better person as a result. As we change our perspective from of course you can't, to of course you can, know and believe that a change is coming. You are what you believe.

THE VISION UNFOLDING

It was finally the holiday time of the year! Everyone that knows me knows that I love Christmas. The weather was around 50 degrees. In Arkansas, you never know the type of weather you will get this time of the year. Just as I didn't know that on December 1, 2012, which was acceptance day to dental schools across the country, I would find myself receiving rejection letters to dental school instead. I had spoken positivity over my life and others. I was receiving many calls from individuals I'd met throughout my internship programs. My initial reaction was to call a friend that I met in my program at The University of Michigan. As I was walking down the sidewalks at The University of Arkansas at Fayetteville, I headed to my dormitory named "The Quads." I did not want to go in just yet. I needed a breath of fresh air. It was a cloudy day with a temperature of about 45 degrees Fahrenheit.

I needed to figure out what was next. Graduation being 5 months away, I immediately needed a plan. As I called my friend, she answered and told me the good news about her acceptance.

"Trice, I am so excited that I just got accepted into dental school! God is so good! Did you get accepted?" she asked.

"Oh my God! That's so amazing!" I said, but deep inside, I felt empty and disappointed.

I was truly happy for her because she and I had both worked hard and sacrificed so much to get accepted, but it was bittersweet for me. I felt discombobulated. I didn't know what I was going to do and quite frankly, I was embarrassed to share with anyone that I didn't get accepted when in my mind, everyone was getting accepted. It didn't make sense to me. There I was, Ms. Positivity, encouraging everyone around me to believe that they would succeed, yet I didn't succeed in getting an acceptance letter. I felt like God was giving me the short end of the stick. I was ashamed that I felt that way, but I was super emotional that all of my hard work had not paid off.

"I knew you would get accepted!" I said, as I fought hard to maintain excitement for her special moment. I sucked up my pride and admitted, "No, to be honest, I didn't get accepted into a program."

"It is okay, Trice! Girl, I have prayed, and God told me that He has something with your name on it. Just wait," she said.

I paused, stopped walking and was at a loss for words.

I replied, "I am not sure if it is possible to get accepted. I have been rejected left and right. I can't get into dental school this cycle. Today was acceptance day."

She laughed and said, "God already told me there is an opportunity with your name on it. You can!"

As I walked back towards my dormitory, I was questioning exactly where and what God had planned for my life. I eagerly wanted to follow His footsteps, but I was losing hope and becoming doubtful. I began to remember the moment…

Of Course, You Can't

2 months prior

"Did you apply to Meharry? You know Dr. Wofford went there?" my mama asked outside of my bedroom door.

I was too congested to answer. Tears flowed down my cheeks as I lay on my bedroom floor, crying, with my face buried in my arms with my eyes on my forearm. Beside my head lay a book with statistics of individuals who would get accepted into dental school based on the particular school's overall acceptance rate and the recommended DAT (Dental Admissions Test) score. The average recommended acceptance score ranged between 18-20. My crumbled Dental Admission Test score report was balled up in my fist with a score of 15.

The thought of not achieving my dream was unbearable. I was physically and mentally weak. I had received more denial letters in the mail than free coupons. I didn't know what I would do next. There was absolutely no way I could have scored this low. I continued to close my eyes, pray, and open them as if the score was going to change.

There was a squeaking noise from my door being opened. I heard my mom's heels walking into the entryway of my bedroom. Suddenly, I felt my mom's presence hovering over me as my face remained towards the floor. My mom stood there in confusion, as it looked as though she had just come home from work. She had her boots on with a computer bag wrapped around her shoulder.

My mom then stated, "God spoke to me and told me that there was a reason that your very first internship was with Dr. Samuel Wofford who attended Meharry back in the 1960's."

I sat up from the floor with the pounding headache that I had, wiped my eyes and told my mom that, "I did not have enough money to apply for another school at that time."

My mom immediately pulled out her debit card and told me she was going to apply to Meharry for me, because God is speaking to her that this was where I was supposed to be. I figured my mom was being hopeful, but then during the encounter with my friend, I realized that God was speaking to me. What exactly was He saying?

December 2012

As I entered my dormitory building on this cold December day, there was a 615 telephone number calling me. I simply wanted to go into my dormitory room, close my door and bundle under my covers with my blinds closed in the twin-sized bed that I had. That is exactly what I did. Until I received a voicemail following the unanswered telephone call. For me, I don't answer unknown calls. I never have, for some reason. I feel like there's always an automatic number calling me and I just never like picking up. Well, this was a similar case but this time, I probably should have answered. As I listened to the voicemail there was a lady from administration at Meharry Medical College who had left a voicemail inviting me for an interview. As I fell to my knees, tears fell from my eyes in overwhelming excitement and puzzlement of what was taking place. My previous conversation with my friend replayed in my mind, mentioning that God already told her that there was an opportunity with my name on it. My mind was blown. I turned on my lights in my dormitory and called the number back.

Before the person on the other end of the telephone could answer, I immediately said, "Yes! This is Ratrice. Did someone call this number for me?"

"Hello Ratrice. Yes, we called to notify you that your application was selected for our Master of Health Sciences program throughout our graduate department. Upon completion, this will secure a seat in our dental school. We hope that you will accept this interview. There is no application process for this master's, but we select applicants that we believe will succeed within our dental school and we will assist in improving the DAT score, and it will be allowed to be retaken at completion of the master's program."

My mouth dropped. I never in my life thought of going to get a master's degree. I was actually confused when I got the call. I had planned to go directly into dental school, but this DAT score was "holding me back." I had been praying for God to work a miracle because at the moment, it looked like my dream to get into dental school was over. I could not pass the test, and I would have had to wait another year to reapply for dental school.

At that moment I knew God was answering my prayers, but His answer was far different from my own. I never would have imagined that a college would randomly *select* me for a Master of Health Sciences program.

I had never heard of this degree or applied for it. But I realized that God was giving me more than I had asked for. Instead of sitting out for a year and letting my mind and skills get rusty, God allowed me to use that year to get a higher level of education while getting the help I needed to pass the DAT.

Immediately, I heard my friend's voice ringing in my head.

"God has something with your name on it"

I thought she was just trying to make me feel better at the time, but sure enough, my name was selected for this master's degree. My name was on the eventual passed Dental Admissions Test. God, indeed, had something with my name on it.

***

Our minds can really make us believe that our dreams are not possible. Just when I felt all hope for getting into dental school was lost, I received a call from an unknown number that led me to my dream of becoming a dentist. Sure, this path would add an additional year of school, but God knows what we need even when we don't. I wanted to go right into dental school, but God knew that I still needed my Master of Health Sciences degree. I realized God was protecting my vision. Have you heard the saying that, "God's rejection is His protection"? I received many rejections to dental school because God was protecting me in order to build and grow me.

Having the feeling that God has forgotten about me is probably a very familiar feeling across the board. But then compare that feeling to when you receive what you have been praying for. That moment where you thought something wasn't possible, but you turned it into an I'M possible. That moment where you turned your can't into a can. I experienced this without knowing what was next for me approaching graduation.

In life, we all experience roadblocks. It is inevitable as humans, and sometimes that pain can change us. As the vision is unfolding for you, allow your setbacks and blocks to be stepping-stones. This is easier said than done. Remembering this moment that I was in, I literally wanted to be in a dark room with my blinds closed unbothered by anyone. Even when my friend mentioned that God had told her that there was a blessing with my name on it, I still didn't believe it. That is crazy to think about, right? How many of you are reading this, and you know that what I am saying is encouraging and inspiring you, but you may not believe that what you are waiting on can happen to you? One of my favorite scriptures that I share with many is Habakkuk 1:5. It reads:

"Look at the nations and watch— and be utterly amazed. For I am going to do something in your days that you would not believe, even if you were told."

I read this verse over and over after I received the telephone call for my interview. A lot of times we wonder why we don't receive that yes when we want, but I believe that if you don't give up, and if you continue to keep your head high, before your eyes you will see your vision...unfolding.

WHAT'RE YOU LISTENING TO?

As thousands of Americans make the walk across a graduation stage, one thing is certain: "Pomp and Circumstance" will be played. There are no lyrics, just the traditional song that is instantly recognized when hearing it played at graduations.

And there I was, graduating from The University of Arkansas at Fayetteville May 2013. I remember the giant presentation of honorary speakers, walking through Bud Walton arena, awaiting my name to be called and wondering to myself, "What's next?" Pomp and Circumstance was still playing in the background but I, too, had background music of my own. My thoughts were rambling, and I was asking myself before anyone else could, "Ratrice, what are your plans now that you've graduated?" I continued to await a call back from the interview at Meharry. I knew that would be the first question asked. I continued through the arena wearing my all black cap and gown with black heels. As my name was called, Ratrice Rochelle Jackson, I got jitters because I knew how much hard work I had put into studying day in and day out. I spent the majority of my time during undergrad either in the library or in the chemistry lab, studying for exam after exam.

These thoughts rambled through my mind as the speaker was speaking. Before I knew it, I turned around and saw my family in the audience screaming,

"Whooooo! Go Ratrice!" Their presence made me smile and there it was - everyone's caps thrown in the air, with confetti dropping from the ceilings to congratulate the graduating class of 2013 Fulbright Arts and Sciences. You know, just like the typical after graduation pictures that are taken which are embodied with the graduation dinner.

Meanwhile, my mind wondered *what was next*. Still no call. Still no answer.

Humans have a daily background music that consists of thoughts that go through our mind over and over again. Sometimes this could be what someone has said to you, a proposed dream, or simply what you think of yourself. There is a variety of background music that is played throughout our minds daily. Sometimes it could be the same thought: positive or negative. Just as though the same graduation song which is played at a graduation that delivers an accomplished moment in life, we have internal music playing as well. Based on a study presented at John Hopkins Medicine Wellness and Prevention, it states, "If you want to keep your brain engaged throughout the aging process, listening to or playing music is a great tool. It provides a total brain workout." Research has shown that listening to music can reduce anxiety, blood pressure, and pain, as well as improve sleep quality, mood, mental alertness, and memory.

So I ask you, what is your background music? What are you listening to? The reality is, some of us may be playing the same song that we have been playing for years. What we tell ourselves and allow to replay over in our brain, I believe, affects everything about us. It certainly did for me. What are you listening to?

THE ART OF BELIEVING

I will never forget the sound of the tambourines clapped in the hands of those at Mt. Calvary: Church of God in Christ in Roe, Arkansas. This is where I went every summer for vacation bible school. As you walked inside of the church, you would also see the hand fans used quite frequently throughout the church service. These hand fans had a popsicle stick glued with hot glue to the back of a paper with the church's photo on the front. I remember always wanting to sit by my grandma, because getting your hands on those church fans in mid-July in Arkansas, when the temperature outside was touching 100 degrees Fahrenheit, was equivalent to winning the lottery. At least, that is what I thought during those moments when I was younger. My family and I called driving down to see my grandma, "going to the country." This trip to the country is about forty-five minutes to an hour from my hometown of Little Rock, Arkansas. In the summertime, it was guaranteed you would find one of my uncles or cousins riding on a John Deere green and yellow lawnmower. Also, the red push mower was used with grass being flung through the air, while the cowboy hat was worn and a white towel covered in sweat was hanging from underneath due to the intense sun. The mosquitoes were terrible, and it was scorching outside. By terrible I mean the mosquitoes came in bulk, ready to bite whatever was in sight. Sometimes I dreaded the summertime for this reason, because I would somehow attain on average twelve mosquito bites per summer.

Well, I drifted off a bit there. I wanted to share that growing up, it was instilled in me the importance of putting God first despite the circumstances. My faith was built at a young age, especially during vacation bible school. My grandma, Juanita Owens, would be our teacher, and my cousins and I would always leave each day with an assignment. Sometimes those assignments consisted of learning bible verses, and other times they included knowing all of the books in the bible, old testament and new testament, by memory. During vacation bible school, we would always encapsulate the scripture and apply it to our daily lives in order to better ourselves.

My grandmother on my mom's side of the family is who we would visit in Roe, Arkansas, and I called her Grandma. My grandmother from my dad's side of the family is who we would visit in DeWitt, Arkansas, and I have always called her Nanny. They were about a 30-minute drive apart. Both of my grandmothers went to high school together. When I found this out, I knew the world was a small world. My mom and dad's mothers were classmates. My grandma and nanny would always make sure that we were constantly putting God first and praying every night.

After vacation bible school was over throughout the week, my family and I would all go back to my grandma's house and watch television and play UNO. It was normally about nine of us who would pack our bags and spend the week in my grandma's four-bedroom house. Whether we made a pile of blankets on the floor, on the couch or staggered in the beds, we knew that we had one another. This was tradition for us.

Even writing this is taking me down memory lane to understanding how blessed we are as humans. I know times have changed and some of you reading may not know what I am referring to, and some may. I say times have changed, because have you ever seen a television that had the antenna at the top? You remember the ones where if it were not pointing in the right direction, the picture would become fuzzy and grainy? Well, my grandma had this television, and there were no cable systems or Wi-Fi. We had about 5 consistent channels that we watched. Those channels included the news and 'The Price is Right.' More or less. My grandma would make sure that we did not run too hard across the kitchen where the television was placed, or there would be broken-down reception due to the antenna being moved out of position. For me, I loved watching NBA basketball. This was usually played on the news channels, so I was able to watch it. I would make sure no one moved too quickly, too, because I wanted to see the outcome of the basketball games I watched.

It was upsetting when the grain would appear on the television because the reception was lost.

With broken-down reception, the image and outcome of the television is not the same. When I thought back to the times of me growing up, I thought about the *art of believing*. It brought me to one of my last days in college, when I was walking to my dormitory and I allowed myself to believe inaccurate truths about myself. Those inaccurate truths that I was feeding myself while the vision was unfolding were that I was not going to get accepted into dental school, and that it was too late because I had not acquired the score that statistics were showing to be acceptable.

That was the day where I needed to adjust my faith and the antenna in my life to get better reception. I tapped into the scriptures I'd learned in those hot vacation bible school classes. Sometimes in life, we have to turn the channel from the undesirable thoughts that we are choosing to believe. Just as meticulously as I went about assuring that the antenna was placed in the correct location at my grandma's house so that the basketball game that I wanted to watch wouldn't be distorted is the same action I believe we should apply to our circumstances. Sometimes we, as humans, are running too fast or not allowing ourselves the patience to allow the antenna in our lives to catch the signal. I believe that how you see yourself is crucial. I always say that life is about perception. Your perception gives rise to your choices and behavior.

Art is the expression or application of human creative skill and imagination, while believing is accepting something as true. When I wrote the art of believing I thought of both of these definitions which described my story. I know that this can relate to you, because as long as you accept something as true, it is just a matter of time before you see that come to fruition.

Two weeks following my graduation from the University of Arkansas, I continued to wait patiently on what was next. I adjusted my antenna in my life to the positivity of my future. As I waited, I had other plans that consisted of working within dentistry.

I was not sure if I would get accepted into the master's program that I interviewed for or not, but I made sure I had a plan that was going to lead me in the right direction. I continued to make connections and talked to others who knew my situation and could help me through. In mid-May, while I was eating a burger in a place with bad reception, I walked outside of the burger place and walked to where I could hear my telephone and, in that moment, I received my acceptance to this program. This process, though, taught me that there are many areas in life where there is bad reception, but though there is bad reception, that does not stop God from making a way for you.

This moment gave me clarity. Of course I was happy and overwhelmed with joy, but I also did not understand why the process had gone that way for me. I was being taught patience and faith, and my connection with Christ increased. My connection with Christ increased tremendously because, in that moment alone, I knew that I could not do this journey called life by myself and through my own will.

I realized that sometimes we may unknowingly be in an area with bad reception, but that keeping the right attitude is what goes a long way. Being able to adjust our own antennas in our lives is something that we may have to do from time to time. When you find yourself in an area physically or mentally where that adjustment is

Of Course, You Can't

needed to increase your faith, or just a readjustment of your mindset, I want you to breathe and know that this is...the art of believing.

FINDING MY PURPOSE

It was 2016, and I was a second-year dental student entering into my third year. I was praying about what God had for me next. I knew that I had a passion to help underserved communities and I also knew that I loved dentistry, but I still wasn't clear on which direction to take with my life or career. When people finish dental school, they typically become general dentists unless they decide to specialize, but I didn't want to work strictly with adults. I was young and felt like I would spend more time trying to convince patients that I was old enough to treat them.

I don't know if I did the right thing; I would think to myself. *Do I really want to be a dentist?*

How frustrating. I had spent the last eight years of my life working for this dream; crying, depriving myself of sleep and food, and I was still questioning myself. Graduating dental school is enough for some, but I just felt like God had so much more for me.

As a third-year dental student, I would have to start my clinical rotations and start working with living patients, and I wanted to be prepared.

I decided to search online for opportunities where I could get more experience when I came across a mission trip for dentists. On the mission trip I would serve the underserved communities in Catadupa, Saint James, Jamaica, for one week. As I read further, I saw that I would have the opportunity to perform extractions, clean teeth, and inject anesthetic into a person's mouth so that they were numb during the procedure. I had never been out of the country. It was on my bucket list to travel but, during this time, I knew that I wanted to travel with purpose. I had spent my previous summers doing mission work with communities in Seattle, Washington, Ann Arbor Michigan, Nashville, Tennessee, and Little Rock, Arkansas, but I had never taken my love and passion to communities abroad.

As a first-timer traveling out of the country, I was privileged to travel with Zion Care International. The mission of this trip was to promote and preserve the health, welfare, and physical well-being of the economically challenged and needy, throughout Jamaica and the world. I was also able to engage in charitable work projects aimed at assisting and empowering individuals in the community, while also providing dental care to children and adults in small towns where access to dental care is almost nonexistent.

When we arrived, I was amazed to find communities of people that had never seen a dentist in their lives. One lady was about 50 years old, and said she had never met a dentist. It was quite a culture shock for me. Many of the necessities that we take for granted in the USA are privileges for them. These people had walked barefoot for miles to come see us. They had never owned more than one toothbrush, and would bathe in the ocean to clean themselves.

It was at this moment that I began to truly appreciate the many blessings in my life; things like electricity and running water. For many of the services I performed, headlights were used to light the dark field where we worked. The conditions were less than ideal and the buildings that were used did not have the luxury of modern technology.

Seeing the thankfulness of children and adults receiving dental care in Jamaica brought tears to my eyes every day. I had a patient who stood up and gave me a hug with tears in her eyes, saying, "Thank you so much for your service, student doc. We have never had anyone come to our community to give us service. Thank you! I will never forget this moment."

This experience reminded me of the many blessings that we have in America that we take for granted. I became more grateful for basic things like shoes and vehicles; even corner stores and restaurants. But I also grew to love the simplicity of these people's lives. Here they were, living in what we in first-world countries would call squalor, but they were so happy. There was no road rage, no pollution or police sirens blaring down the roads like in the big cities. It was in this stillness that I was able to hear God's voice clearly.

One day, while enjoying the sounds of the large ocean waves crashing on the shore and the sun blazing over the beautiful Jamaican landscape, God spoke to me, saying, "This is what you should be doing."

Then and there, I knew that my place was to serve children. I would specialize in pediatric dentistry. God showed me a bigger vision than just cleaning teeth. He wanted me to impact families through the medium of dentistry. God showed me that pediatric dentistry opened the door for me to not only change the lives of children, but the lives of the parents too. I would use my platform as a pediatric dentist to not only improve oral health, but speak words of encouragement and empowerment daily.

My world changed for the better. There is no greater feeling in this life than knowing that you are doing exactly what God has created you to do. I encourage all people to seek that true calling. Walk in the purpose for which God has created you.

The success of my dental mission was not measured by the dental care I provided or my ability to practice my craft, but by being able to interact with people from another culture and help the underserved. This experience opened my eyes to the many families living in poverty who lack access to basic health care. Now I seek opportunities and experiences which allow me to help and improve the quality of life of others. It is my mission to give back to communities that look like me. I am driven to improve the health of the underserved.

I share this story as insight to the bridge that led me to where I am today. We may all have those ever-changing moments in our lives when the light bulb turns on and shines bright with inspiration. That light bulb for me, someone from Arkansas, was knowing that I was going to do everything that I could do to positively impact the lives of children and adults.

***

After discovering my purpose in Jamaica, I came back home excited and believing that things would progress smoothly. No more struggling. No more failing exams.

God had told me to become a pediatric dentist, so things would become easy, right? Wrong! Little did I know, the biggest storm of my life was heading my way.

Let's be real. We all know life isn't easy. We all are going through some form of adversity by the season and some by the day, to the point where we may even become mad at God. Sometimes it feels like you can't catch a break. Even writing this in 2021, I reflect on 2020 and what an absurd year it was. I mean come on, in 2020 we experienced a worldwide pandemic because of a virus named Covid-19 that took people's lives left and right and still is doing.

If you're a believer, I know you understand that feeling where you are praying and even working towards your goals, and nothing seems to change. I have felt that. It makes you feel weak and it makes you wonder "why?" Why me? You ask those questions to God and you may even start to look at others and not understand how they have it "easier" than you. Truth is, this is what we call life; those moments where you want to be alone in a room screaming and crying with your face buried in a pillow.

We have those moments where we say, "Dang, I really can't take this anymore." The word "can't" begins to float in our vocabulary, and then our mind starts believing it and bringing it into our reality. I know how difficult it is to turn "can't" into "can." I know that it can be challenging to stay positive and see the good in the world when nothing seems to be going in a favorable direction for you.

Sometimes we don't want to tell our stories because they are far too painful. However, this is often the best time to tell the story. Many times we feel as though we must master our challenges before we can tell our stories. We celebrate the outcome over the process. When we are in the midst of what looks like failure, we isolate ourselves and hide the truth, waiting for the day when we can come out and share how we overcame it. That is exactly how I felt before writing this book. But I now realize the power of sharing my weakest and most vulnerable experience.

Being vulnerable about your situation isn't easy. It's not easy for me right now writing this, but I knew that I wanted to take the time to share my story to help people who are experiencing the same trauma. The next chapter is about the biggest storm of my life.

BE STILL

For nearly a year - three hundred and thirty long, exhausting days - I was listening for God yet hearing nothing but silence and you've *failed*....again. I was growing sour, angry, and pessimistic. Being raised in a praying family, I knew the enemy would test me with trials and tribulations. I knew my faith would be tried. From the moment I spoke into the universe, "Yes, I can!" I had a feeling that I would have to confront obstacles, but after hearing from God, I thought those tests were over.

Instead, I felt like I couldn't catch a break. I had taken the National Board Dental Examination Part II and failed. Yet another extremely important exam unsuccessfully taken. I could not believe that I'd studied for so long and still I would look into my results and see: *fail*.

I just wanted to graduate from dental school, but it seemed like everything that could go wrong, did go wrong. Even though I had heard God's voice less than a year prior, my faith began to waiver. How could I be a dentist if I couldn't pass the test?

I knew I needed to make some adjustments somewhere. I continued to believe in God because I knew that He would not fail me, but I also knew that I needed to alter my studying to improve in areas that needed it the most.

Three months later, I took the examination for the second time. I was in my senior year and I had been selected to interview for residency programs. I was super excited to get interviews. I applied to nine programs and was asked to interview at six of them. Sheesh! That was pretty good. I did not have an example of what it looked like to be successful at matching into these residency programs. I was determined to be that example for other African American students who decided to walk this path.

Across the world, most programs on average accepted four to five residents. It was pretty intense. If I did not gain an acceptance, then I would have to try again another year. During my very first interview at the NYU Langone-Missouri site, my mom and dad said that they would drive me there from my hometown of Little Rock, Arkansas. I was a ball of emotions as we drove to Missouri. I was happy and excited to have the opportunity to interview, but I was also nervous because the results from my big exam were coming as well. Mind you, I had to pass this exam in order to graduate and receive my Doctor of Dental Surgery degree and in order to matriculate into a residency program.

My interview went well, and everything was fantastic until the interview was over. Following the interview there was an hour's gap until the dinner to thank interviewees for attending. During that hour, I was filled with anxiety and my stomach started to hurt as I worried about the results of my exam. I decided to take a nap. My parents did not think much of it because it had been a long day. I laid my phone on the floor next to the bed. When I woke up, I was afraid to pick up my phone.

How embarrassing could it be to know that I failed again? I need to pass this exam to get into residency, I thought to myself.

My palms were sweating, and I could barely nap.

Forget it, I thought.

After summoning the courage, I snatched the phone from the floor. My fingers trembled as I typed in my login information to access my scores.

There it was.... FAIL

***

No, wait? Are you serious? I literally studied so much for this exam, I thought.

I wanted to scream, but my parents were in the room watching television. I had to hold myself together. I actually pinched myself to make sure that it was real. I could feel the tears ready to burst from my eyes, so I rushed to the bathroom.

My dad asked, "Hey baby! Do you need me to iron your clothes for dinner?"

"No Sir, I'm good," I replied, hoping to hide the pain in my voice.

What a horrible feeling. It was November and I was six months away from graduation with one more attempt left to take my exam. I was sick to my stomach. It was like running a race while out of breath, knowing that I was nowhere near the finish line, but that I couldn't quit. I needed a mental break. This was more than not passing an exam. I literally didn't know if I would be able to graduate.

Eight years of studying and sacrifice for what?

I had three months to prepare for my final attempt to pass this exam. Words cannot express the fear that consumed me. If I failed this third attempt, it would be GAME OVER! Time up! No do-overs! This would have been the last time I could take the exam in a lifetime. If I failed again, I would not finish my doctorate program and would not be able to work as a licensed dentist.

The $100,000 per year I was taking out in loans for dental school would have just been a nice contribution to Meharry Medical College. Can you imagine that? I knew that I was taking out unimaginable amounts of loans every year for dental school, but I didn't truly appreciate the risk I was taking until it was all on the line. Imagine owing over $300,000 for school and walking away with no degree and not having the opportunity to try again. I had literally staked my financial future on becoming a dentist. Would I leave this program with nothing to show for it?

I put in so much hard work. I truly did. Late nights, late studying, praying. But what did I have to show for that aside from an exam that was holding me back? The time, effort, perseverance, and passion. I started to lose sight because of the outcome of the results. How many times can you see a failure before you give up? How many times can you see a failure before you say, "I can't do it, this isn't for me."

I had failed the second test with only slight improvements, even after committing to a strict study regime. What else could I do? What would be different for the third test? My mother and I immediately began searching for programs that could help me. Either the programs were too expensive, charging as high as $2,000 per session, or they did not work for my schedule.

My mother was willing to pay $2,000 for tutoring. She's a great mother and would do anything to see me succeed, but I had to draw the line somewhere. I was living on loans already. I couldn't add this additional expense to my parents.

"I'm not doing all that Mama! That's too much."

"Well, do you have any classmates who passed the test?" Mama asked.

"Yes. There's a guy we call P.T. He is one of the top tutors in the school, but he doesn't tutor for the board exam."

"It's worth a try. Just ask him. Tell him we'll pay him."

I agreed. What was the worst that could happen? The next day, I called P.T. The phone rang and I nearly hung up. The shame of telling someone that I had failed this test began to hover over me like a dark cloud. I forced myself to stay on the phone. I needed to pass this test more than I needed to look good in the eyes of strangers.

"Hello?" P.T. said in his gentle accent.

"Hey P.T.! This is Ratrice," I said with a cracked voice. I waited to see if he recognized me.

"Hello Ratrice!"

"Hey, P.T. I was calling to see if you could help me." I began to choke up as I was about to utter the painful words. "I can't pass the National Board Exam, and I really need some help."

I'm sure he could hear the pain in my voice.

"Okay. Tell me what you have been using to study."

"I've done everything!" I said in a panic. "I've used the Dental Decks, different NBDE Part II Apps, Mosby's NBDE Book, flash cards, you name it. I have done this numerous times. I don't know what else to do!" Tears were rolling down my face.

P.T. agreed to tutor me, and I thanked him profusely.

For the next three months, P.T. and I studied daily. One day P.T. asked me to attend Temple with him. "I want to pray for God to help me as a tutor for you. I believe this is what I am meant to do."

I was feeling so much better about taking this third exam. P.T. was the best tutor in the school, and he was even praying for even more skills to tutor me with. I had all the gods helping me. I just knew I was going to pass.

Three months passed quickly, but I felt prepared. I had taken the test twice before and just received tutoring from the best. How could I not pass? Scores were sent out three weeks after, but I was already celebrating and telling everyone of my success, even before I knew my scores. I was getting gifts from people congratulating me on passing the exam. I could have been a float at the Macy's Thanksgiving Day Parade, my head was blown up so large!

Match Day was coming up. Match Day is where students across the world get accepted to or rejected from their specialty programs. This was a very intense and competitive process. This is like the NBA Draft of dentistry. I was so ready to tell the world,

"I've decided to take my talents to Tampa Bay, Florida."

It was 6:45 a.m. when I got the email.

"Your Dental Match Result!" the subject line read!

I closed my eyes before opening it, and when I opened the email, it read:

"Congratulations, you have matched! You have been matched to:

Institution: NYU Luthern-Tampa, FL

Program: Pediatric Dentistry-2 YR- Tampa, FL"

I jumped out of bed screaming with delight. I'd matched into my #1 residency program choice.

Seriously? Wow, I thought to myself when I found out. I was bursting with joy. Life just felt like it was all coming together. I had never drunk champagne early in the morning, but that day, I popped the bubbly!

Two weeks later, I woke up eager to log into my student portal. My exam results would be posted, and I would finally see the words I had been fighting for. I snatched my phone from the dresser so quickly it almost flew out of my hand. After fumbling the phone around and securing a firm grasp, I hurriedly typed in my username and password with a smile so big my cheeks hurt.

There it was: Click for Results

I pushed the icon on my screen and waited impatiently for the page to buffer. The words slowly appeared:

FAIL

***

No tears. No words. Just empty.

My hands went limp and my phone fell to the floor. My face was emotionless. I was numb all over. My room-

Of Course, You Can't

mate walked over in concern. She must have thought I was having a stroke.

"Girl, what's wrong?" she asked.

She picked up my phone to find the huge "FAIL" on the screen.

No words...

She was in just as much shock as I was. Being a dental student, she understood that I had just met the end of the tracks for my dental career.

"I don't even know what to say to you. I'm so sorry."

My mind could not process this moment. I laid down and went to sleep.

I woke up crying in hysteria. I was angry and frantic. What kind of evil game was God playing with me? I had just matched with my first choice for a specialty program. There were people who passed the exam on the first try who didn't match, let alone match with their school of choice.

How on earth does this make sense?

I really thought that God was torturing me. I grew entirely angry at God. How hard would it have been for God to help me remember one single question on the exam? I wasn't asking for a miracle. I just needed to pass a test, not raise the dead. Why had He forsaken me? He told me to become a pediatric dentist, but I failed the test and would never be able to take it again.

What do you do when it looks like all hope is gone?

I did not know what life ahead of me would look like. The hope I had inside of me grew slender. The thought of possibly walking across the stage and not receiving my degree and not being told *yes, you can* become a pediatric dentist was too much to bear. I was done. I mean done.

I had trusted in God and I felt for years straight that I was being let down. A variety of emotions overturned, and my mind started playing tricks on me. I cried my eyes out and didn't know what it felt like to be happy anymore. I started to take life at my own will and trust in my own self, because I felt that I'd have a better chance at not letting myself down. I got tired of my muscles being tight, pounding heartbeats, feeling lonely, hopeless…lost.

See, there's nothing perfect about the storm when it's happening. When I think back on this moment in my life, I wanted to share it with you, because similar to the tree that needs sunlight, we also need water. We all appreciate the beautiful sunshine and cooling breeze, but we hate the storm. We get so distracted by the dark clouds and violent winds that we ignore the life-giving water that the storm provides. I was focusing so much on the storm that I let it crumble me down to pieces, but that storm was necessary for my growth and development.

The enemy wanted me to believe that it was time to give up. I had resigned myself to the idea that if it was meant to be, then it would not have been so hard. I walked to my dean's office with tears running down my face. My roommate had suggested I request that the dean write a letter on my behalf, requesting another attempt. I knew this was impossible. So many people have failed this test and walked away with nothing; they were not going to change the rules because I was upset. I didn't know what I was going to say to the dean. Something just compelled me to at least talk to her.

***

"I need to see the dean," I asked.

I was shaking, my eyes were beet red, and my skin was flushed.

"Do you have an appointment?"

I was trying to explain why I was there, but I was crying so hard that she could not understand what I was saying.

"Just have a seat! I'll go get her," she said.

After a few minutes, Dean Black came walking out with her arms outstretched. Without saying a word, she wrapped me in her arms and allowed me to cry. After I composed myself, I explained.

"I failed my board exam. I'm not going to be able to become a dentist."

"Don't worry. As long as you are a Meharrian, you will get through this," she said, thinking that they were encouraging me to try again.

"No! You don't understand," I said. "I took the test for the third time. I can't take it anymore. It's over!" I began to cry again. I was inconsolable. Dr. Black and the assistant dean had no words. They allowed me to sit in the office for hours. After a couple of hours, the assistant dean hastily came out of his office.

"Wait a minute! Let me check something out!" he said, rushing out of the room.

After a few minutes he came back in with a huge grin on his face.

"Student Doctor Jackson, it looks like you're in luck. Just last month, the rules were changed. As of January, students are now able to attempt the test…."

He paused for dramatic effect

"FIVE TIMES!!"

My bad knees nearly gave out! But not because of my injuries this time.

"Is this a joke?" I screamed. "Am I getting another chance to take the exam?"

"Yes you are!" Dean Black said.

God had literally worked a miracle. I was going to be able to take the test again. I still had a chance to become a dentist!

***

The year of 2017 was one of great physical pain and intense emotional distress. I lost over 20 pounds from the stress. I experienced two surgeries, I was in the emergency room with a traumatic episode of kidney stones, and my grandmother passed away. It seems like I had cried every day to pass my exam, only to fail.

Why would God let me experience such an exhausting experience? Every time I failed the examination, I had to wait another ninety days to try again. I spent every single day in between re-studying for the examination. I did not understand why God was not answering my prayers.

God was bringing me closer and closer to him throughout these events, but I felt like I was all alone. It reminded me of the poem *Footprints in the Sand.* In this poem, a man is walking on the beach with Jesus. He takes notice of the two sets of footprints. But when the waters were crashing the worst, the poet wrote that he looked back and saw one set of footprints. He questioned Jesus and asked why Jesus had left him alone when the waves were crashing at their worst, but Jesus explained to him that it was at those times where Jesus was carrying the poet. The single set of footprints was Jesus'.

One day, I reached out to my sister for counsel. As she answered my Facetime, I instantly saw a sign on her wall that read, "Be still and know that I am God." I opened my eyes immensely because that was the same quote that Mrs. Mary Porter had sent me that same morning. Mrs. Mary is my mom and dad's friend and she sends me Bible scriptures every day of the year, without fail. On this day, it stuck with me. I was asking God for a sign; I was actively searching for an ear for someone to hear my pain and desire to simply *pass* my examination.

God was showing me what I needed to see. He said, "Ratrice, Be Still." Chills ran through my body, tears slowly came from my eyes and I then knew that God was listening. For the first time in eight years, I was at complete peace. My soul rested. When I took the exam for the fourth time, I didn't know if I would pass or fail, but I was at peace.

Being still is the art of remaining in place, free from sound or noise or the state of being silent. Jesus also used the term "be still" to stop chaos, anxiety, and stress. When the waves were beating against the boat that He and the disciples were in, Jesus said, "Peace, be still." God calmed the raging beast of ambition within me. He showed me that I had to trust in Him alone. I had to be still and allow Him to open the doors of success in my life.

I believe sometimes in life it is easier to think that God is not listening to our prayers or hearing us, but actually we never allow God time to finish His work.

"Be Still", He said. "Be Still."

OF COURSE, YOU CAN

Chances are this isn't your first-time hearing someone say, "Of course, you can." I'm also sure that this isn't the first time you've come across a motivational book or that someone has encouraged you through a tough time. It's good to have those situations where you're able to bounce back because of an inspiring message or simply due to someone believing in you. There is a certain comfort from watching someone else's story or hearing it and saying, "They're so blessed!"

In reflection, I would always hear the saying, "God is writing your story," but quite frankly, I never knew what that meant. It's always easier to believe and say that you can do whatever you put your mind to when things are going well. But whew, when Murphy's Law hits you, you'll be questioning yourself and searching for that motivation before your eyes can blink.

For me, it started in 2017 when I kept failing the National Board Dental examination. This exam was five hundred dollars each time that I took it. So, I spent about two thousand dollars simply on re-taking examinations. You know when you're in school, money doesn't grow on trees, so this was an instance where it hurt to swipe that card and give someone my money without knowing the outcome.

Of course, I hoped for the best, but with how everything was playing out, it seemed like my card was a walking magnet of withdrawals due to exams. I finally passed the exam on my fourth attempt, right before my dental school graduation in May of 2018, but my journey was far from over. I immediately had to enroll in my patient examination in order to get licensed to practice dentistry. This experience was a rodeo.

I was mentally and physically exhausted. I couldn't tell myself that I was exhausted though, because I was about to begin a pediatric dental residency program. This was a two-year program and I knew that the road would be tough, because I still had to take the licensure examination in order to practice dentistry following completion of my residency. I promise you, I never want to take another test in my life! I would always tell my mom,

"Mama, when this is all said and done, I will have probably spent ten thousand dollars on exams alone."

I felt behind, delayed, denied, and saddened because my co-residents were already licensed. They had already completed their written board exams and the patient licensure exam in dental school before residency. I, on the other hand, still had to pass these exams and successfully complete my residency.

I was exhausted. I was in school for my residency from 7a.m - 5:00 p.m. and then I had to rush to Tampa General Hospital for mandated emergency rotations from 5:00 pm – 11: 00 pm. Though my days consisted of 12-hour workdays throughout the residency program, I spent whatever time I needed to practice until the exam. In those moments I would organize my 24-hour days and take full advantage of my time. My co-residents were amazed at how I balanced a full workload schedule, and I was on the line of re-taking an exam that would enable me to be completely licensed.

I walked through life every day completely happy and pretty much calm.

"How do you stay so calm through your struggle, Ratrice?" my co-resident asked.

"I know things will work out how they're supposed to!" I responded.

"I don't understand how you do that. I am so exhausted every day since coming to residency," she sighed.

I didn't tell them, but I was more exhausted than them. It was the "stillness" that gave me strength through the journey. I realized that it was never my power; it was the patience I allowed myself to have through the wait. It was pretty ridiculous to me, but I kept my head high. I didn't really have a choice. Sometimes, when you reach the crossroads, you decide whether you stop or you keep pushing. I had experienced so much turmoil through the storm and rain that I learned to fully put my trust in God and to be still.

***

May 5, 2019, was my final attempt at the live patient exam.

I had to find a volunteer who would allow me to conduct live dental work for a pass or fail grade. If I failed, that would mean I did *not* properly treat them, and they would have to go home with a bad filling in their mouths. The pressure was extreme. The exam consists of 1 crown and 1 root canal on a manikin, and the second section consists of two different types of fillings on a live patient and a deep cleaning. If you do not meet their criteria - for example, if your dental prep does not fall into the category of a pass, then you would fail and have to retake the entire portion of the exam. Meaning, you pay another $2,000. No matter how great you felt you were at doing fillings and removing cavities, anxiety would hit the fan.

I was a mental, emotional, and physical wreck. My residency program pushed me harder than I had ever been pushed. I had come so far and broken down so many barriers. I didn't know if I could take another disappointment. This would be the final barricade. I could feel the pressure building in my chest as I walked into the dental operatory. My volunteer gave me a nervous grin. I returned the same.

"Lord, please don't let me hurt this man," I silently prayed.

I took a deep breath and dug deep to find the confidence to push forward. I thought about my previous experiences of failure, and I knew that I was going to pay attention to the signs that God had sent to me.

"Be still."

I whispered these words over and over. If I failed the exam, I would have had to re-take all the steps over again. There were a total of 5 steps. I needed 1 more step and if I did not pass this step, every step would have to be retaken, on top of paying another two thousand dollars to register. A peace came over me.

As I worked on my volunteer, I was so confident. I knew that I was doing my best and that I was walking with God. People in the room were looking at me like I was crazy. They couldn't understand why I didn't wear the look of worry and stress on my face. I had given in completely to God's will for my life.

My storms opened my eyes to realize that I will never be exempt from adversity. Every day will come with new blessings and new storms. There is a myriad of justifiable reasons to sit back and complain. I spent so much time asking God, "Why me?" But at that moment, I had found complete peace. God reminded me of all of the signs He had given me throughout my journey. He took me back to our conversation in Jamaica where He told me I would be a pediatric dentist and use my platform to speak life into children and adults. My heart filled with joy as I worked on my volunteer patient. I knew that if I continued to stay prayed up and believe, I would be where I was supposed to be.

"We're all done!" I said to my volunteer.

I sent my volunteer to the examiners so that they could check the work.

Ten minutes later, I checked my student portal...

"I passed?"

***

I sat in my car and looked at my results. *PASS*. Written in all caps.

Tears of joy rolled down my face as I burst into ecstatic laughter. Chills ran all over my body because I knew at that moment that this was a lesson. A lesson of faith and many tests. A lesson to show me who is in control. I knew that God was in control of my destiny, and I never wanted to step in the way of that. I knew that everything that I believed for, I would pray and wait on Him. I would always work hard.

I could finally breathe!

Is this how it feels to breathe with no worries? I thought to myself. For three years in a row I was living in a constant storm of worry and stress about examinations. What is your storm? Are you allowing your storm to get in the way of where you want to go? Are you comparing your storm to the next man's storm?

On the other side of the storm, there is something being created. That storm for me was strengthening me for something bigger. You never know when a storm will come. Sometimes the meteorologist can give you the forecast, but it isn't always accurate. I want you to take a moment to think about a time when you faced uncertainty; a moment that made you feel like you "can't." I want you to believe for yourself that your innovation will be released.

***

It was dark outside when I randomly woke up from my sleep. This was unusual for me. I'm always exhausted, so I sleep like a log throughout the night.

What time is it? I wondered. *5:00 a.m.? It's too early!*

The notification over my email icon caught my attention. I had an email.

The sender read: National Dental Association Foundation.

"On behalf of the National Dental Association Foundation: Colgate Palmolive, we would like to congratulate you as our scholarship recipient."

I had applied for this scholarship a year prior. I had forgotten that my application was even in the process. They notified me that I would receive a check in the mail. I was so happy because I was so broke. I had spent so much money over the previous three years. I opened the regular hand-sized envelope and saw a check of 1.. wait, was that 10? $10,000? I sat there dazed. I had been stressing over the past year that I had spent almost ten thousand dollars on my exams and my mom would always say:

"God will restore everything you lost."

This can't be real, I thought.

Walking in what God had for me was a true test of faith. The same exact month, I received the American Academy of Pediatric Dentistry Resident Recognition Award. How could someone with so much struggle and someone who was so "behind" be in a position to receive so many awards?

God showed me that we are never behind when we are walking in His purpose. No one can take away what God has for us, no matter how far behind you may feel you are. My strength, patience and faith were built through the many circumstances and challenges. Through my experiences, *"can't"* began to drift out of my vocabulary. I learned, firsthand, that God can make a way for anyone who believes. Even when your belief seems to be out of this world.

I can do whatever I put my mind to, and I can't wait to share my story with the world, I thought.

I always had an aim and the focus to motivate and inspire others. Everyone has a different story, but everyone has a story. This is my testament for you - to continue believing big and knowing that through your situation, God has the final say.

***

I walked around my residency program and believed like never before.

"I am going to have my own office, once we finish residency, run it, and this is how much money I want to make in the first year," I exclaimed.

"Well, don't get your hopes up. That doesn't happen, especially out of residency," one of my attendings responded.

"Why not? I believe that I can do that. I am not sure how or where, but I know that I can receive this out of residency."

My attending chuckled in my face. He later explained to me, "You can only expect to get paid a certain amount and running your own practice under someone out of residency doesn't typically happen."

Maybe this is our moment to realize that we can't escape the extent of someone's belief, and sometimes we realize that we can't escape where our mind can take us during moments of doubt. But we have a choice. We have the choice to keep believing. A lot of times life will always show you the many reasons why you should agonize over your current situation. The same applies to speaking positivity through your situations.

Of Course, You Can't

No longer let anything keep you from God's best. I am speaking more fulfillment, satisfaction, and success in your life than you have ever dreamed. Don't wait any longer.

Sometimes being strong is the only thing that's left. It's the only choice that you have. You choose. You decide. Never let the next man write your story. Never let society tell you what you can't do. When you're in the moment of battling with your mind and your mind begins to dwell in the midst of an unpleasant feeling, allow yourself to feel. While allowing yourself to feel, challenge your mind to remain strong and believe the positive. Continue to believe the good. Your story is already written. My story is one I wanted and needed to share with you. I knew that I needed to put it all out on paper.

God revealed that to me when I walked into my own dental office at the age of twenty-nine on August 24th, 2020-- you know, the one that someone told me doesn't happen. I know it is not by accident that I passed all of my major examinations on the 24th of 2014, 2018, 2019. I don't believe that it is by accident that my office is located on *Story* road and I live on *Victory* street.

Tell your story. Be victorious. Walk in your why. Believe in your why. Trust in your why. And when the time comes where you are faced with your storm, I want you to look at yourself in the mirror. Now, close your eyes. What you see in the mirror may not always be what you see when your eyes are closed. Allow your belief to start from within. So, now I leave you with this. Which one do you believe? Of course, you can...

www.ingramcontent.com/pod-product-compliance
Lightning Source LLC
Chambersburg PA
CBHW030913080526
44589CB00010B/284